# Eye, Eye, Captain!

JANE CLARKE

ILLUSTRATED BY JENNIE POH

BLOOMSBURY EDUCATION

LONDON   OXFORD   NEW YORK   NEW DELHI   SYDNEY

BLOOMSBURY EDUCATION
Bloomsbury Publishing Plc
50 Bedford Square, London, WC1B 3DP, UK

BLOOMSBURY, BLOOMSBURY EDUCATION and the Diana logo are
trademarks of Bloomsbury Publishing Plc

First published in Great Britain in 2008 by A & C Black, an imprint of Bloomsbury Publishing Plc
This edition published in 2018 by Bloomsbury Publishing Plc

Text copyright © Jane Clarke, 2008
Illustrations copyright © Jennie Poh, 2018

Jane Clarke and Jennie Poh have asserted their rights under the Copyright,
Designs and Patents Act, 1988, to be identified as Author and Illustrator of this work

A catalogue record for this book is available from the British Library

ISBN: PB: 978-1-4729-5055-0; ePDF: 978-1-4729-5648-4; ePub: 978-1-4729-5647-7

2 4 6 8 10 9 7 5 3 1

Printed and bound in China by Leo Paper Products, Heshan, Guangdong

To find out more about our authors and books visit www.bloomsbury.com
and sign up for our newsletters

# Chapter One

The sun was rising over the sea.
On board the *Barracuda*,
seven fierce-looking
pirates were getting
ready to set sail.

Captain Cutlass was leaning against the wheel, trying to read his compass.
"Glasses!" squawked the parrot on his shoulder.
"Hold yer beak, Peggle!" said Captain Cutlass.
Peggle grabbed her beak with her claw.

Captain Cutlass put on his turtle-shell glasses and checked the compass. Peggle removed her claw. "Glasses, glasses, glasses," she squawked softly, nibbling the captain's gold earring.

"Shhhhh!" said the captain. "It's our little secret, remember! If the crew find out I need to wear glasses, they'll make me walk the plank!"

A huge pirate with
an enormous, red beard stomped up.
"What were you saying about glasses,
cap'n?" asked Fearsome Fergus politely,
scratching his beard with his hook.

Captain Cutlass quickly put his glasses
in to his pocket. He smoothed his jacket
over his tubby tummy, grabbed his
cutlass and turned around. "I said,
'pirates don't wear glasses!'"
"Aye, aye, cap'n!" said Fearsome Fergus,
and he went off to tell the others.
Peggle sighed and fluffed up her feathers.

7

The sun rose over the *Barracuda*'s bow. Captain Cutlass put on his pirate hat and called the crew together. He held up a tattered map in one hand and his cutlass in the other. "This is a map of Treasure Island!" he said. "And we're off to find it!"

"Aye, aye, cap'n!" roared the pirates, who were struggling to keep the sun out of their eyes.

Salty Sally put on her sunglasses.
"Take them off!" said Fearsome Fergus.
"If the captain sees, he'll make you walk
the plank! He says pirates don't wear
glasses!"

Salty Sally trembled, and her pigtail
drooped. She quickly took off her
sunglasses. "Sorry," she said. "But I
don't think he saw me."

She was right. Captain Cutlass
was pointing towards the
rising sun with his cutlass.
"Raise the anchor,
me hearties!" he said.
"Treasure Island's
that-a-way!"

# Chapter Two

In the middle of the day, in the middle of the ocean, a huge albatross flew across the sky. It cast its shadow over the *Barracuda*. "Where did that cloud come from?" said Captain Cutlass.

# SPLAT!

"Boggle me eyeballs! It's smelly, white rain!" he said.

"Glasses!" squawked the parrot.

"Hold yer beak, Peggle!" said Captain Cutlass. "Pirates don't wear glasses!"

Peggle sighed and rolled her eyes.

The *Barracuda* was white and sticky.
Captain Cutlass turned to his crew.
"Swab the decks, yer scurvy
scallywags!" he roared.
"Aye, aye, cap'n!" said the pirates.
Then they set to work in the hot,
bright sun.

Salty Sally put on her sunglasses.
"Take them off!" said Fearsome Fergus.
"If the captain sees, he'll make you walk
the plank! He says pirates don't wear
glasses."
"Sorry, I forgot!" said Salty Sally.
"But I don't think he saw me."

The pirates were busy scrubbing the
decks. No one noticed the tentacles
slithering up the side of the ship. A giant
squid was trying to sink the *Barracuda*!

"This seaweed gets everywhere," said the captain, as he walked along the deck. He prodded a mass of waving tentacles with his cutlass.

"Glasses!" squawked the parrot.
"Hold yer beak, Peggle!" said Captain Cutlass. "Pirates don't wear glasses!"
Peggle sighed and covered her eyes with a wing.

The *Barracuda* was covered with slimy
tentacles.
"Clear the decks, yer lily-livered
layabouts!" roared Captain Cutlass.
"Aye, aye, cap'n!" said the pirates.
Then they began to wrestle with the
giant squid.

"There's no stopping us now, Peggle,"
said Captain Cutlass. "Treasure Island
here we come!"
Peggle peeped out from under her wing.
She watched the pirates struggling
with the tentacles. Then she sighed and
covered her eyes again.

# Chapter Three

Late that afternoon, the pirates were pulling off the last of the tentacles when **WHUMP!** the *Barracuda* ran into an enormous whale.

"Boggle me eyeballs!" said Captain Cutlass. "Another pirate ship! It must be the *Jolly Jonah* trying to get to Treasure Island, too."

"Glasses!" squawked the parrot.

"Hold yer beak, Peggle!" said Captain Cutlass. "Pirates don't wear glasses!" Peggle sighed and shrugged her feathers.

The pirates were staring at the whale.
"Board that ship, yer motley mongrels!"
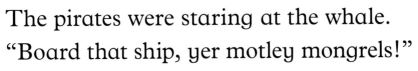
roared Captain
Cutlass.
No one moved.
"Don't just
stand there!
Follow me!"
The captain
grabbed hold of a rope
tied to the mast and
swung across to the
whale. Peggle
clung tightly
on to his
shoulder.

The whale's tail sent Captain Cutlass and Peggle spinning through the air. They landed in the crow's-nest as the whale sank beneath the waves.

Peggle settled back on the captain's shoulder and fluffed up her feathers. "Glasses!" she squawked. There was no one in the crow's-nest, so the captain put on his glasses and looked around. "Glasses, glasses, glasses!" Peggle squawked softly, nibbling the captain's gold earring.

25

"Shhh!" said Captain Cutlass. He put his glasses in to his pocket and called down to the crew. "We sank the *Jolly Jonah*!" The pirates looked at each other.

"And I can see Treasure Island!" the captain went on. "It's over there!" "Arrrrrrr! Treasure Island!" cheered the pirates.

Captain Cutlass climbed down the rigging with Peggle on his shoulder. "Stow the sails, me hearties!" he roared. "Land ahoy!" "Aye, aye, cap'n!" said the pirates.

# Chapter Four

SWOOOSH!

CRUNCH!

THUNK!

The *Barracuda* ran aground on
Treasure Island. The pirates climbed
down on to the sand.

Captain Cutlass took out the treasure map and tried to read it.

"Glasses!" squawked the parrot. "Hold yer beak, Peggle," said Captain Cutlass. "Do I have to keep telling you? Pirates don't wear glasses. If the crew find out, they'll make me walk the plank!"

He turned to his crew. "Dig here!" he ordered, pointing to a spot with his cutlass. "No, here! No, I mean here!"

Peggle sighed and stuck her head under her wing.

The setting sun sparkled on the sea.
Salty Sally put on her sunglasses.
"Take them off!" said Fearsome Fergus.
"Do I have to keep telling you? If the
captain sees, he'll make you walk the
plank! He says pirates don't wear
glasses!"

"OK..." said
Salty Sally.
"But I don't
think the captain
sees anything
much, do you?"

Three days later, there were more holes
in Treasure Island than in a Swiss
cheese, and the pirates still hadn't
found any treasure.

The crew of the *Barracuda* were sweaty, frazzled and dazzled.
The pirates had all had enough.

Salty Sally was sulking.
Fearsome Fergus's face
was as red as his beard.

"You're a crummy, clueless captain!" barked Fearsome Fergus. "You can't tell an albatross from a cloud. You can't tell a giant squid's tentacles from seaweed. You can't tell a whale from a pirate ship. You can't even read a treasure map! If you don't think of something quick, we're going to make you and your moth-eaten parrot walk the plank!"

"Arrrrrrrr! The plank!"
roared the pirates.

Captain Cutlass and Peggle looked at one another and gulped.

"Glasses!" they squawked together.

"Eye, eye, cap'n!" roared the pirates.
And as the captain put on his glasses,
Salty Sally, Fearsome Fergus and all
the pirates put on their sunglasses, too.

"Boggle me eyeballs!" said Captain
Cutlass. "Pirates *do* wear glasses!"

# Chapter Five

Captain Cutlass looked carefully
at the treasure map.

"Well, I never!" he said.
"I've been holding it upside down
all this time!" He turned the map
the right way up. "Glasses, glasses,
glasses," squawked the parrot.

"Aye, Peggle," said Captain Cutlass.
"It's easy to see when you're wearing
glasses. This is where X marks
the spot. Right here, under my
feet!" Then he put down
the map and his cutlass,
and picked up a spade.

Peggle perched in a palm tree, and the
pirates sat in the sunshine and sang
sea shanties. They watched Captain
Cutlass get sweatier and sweatier as he
dug deeper and deeper... and deeper...
until...

**CLUNK!** His spade hit something. Captain Cutlass wiped the sand off his glasses. "I can see a chest!" he yelled. "A treasure chest! Come and help me, yer lazy lumps!"

"Aye, aye, cap'n!" roared the pirates. Then they leapt to their feet.

The sun was setting as the
sweaty pirates heaved and
pulled the treasure chest
out of the hole.

Peggle flew to Captain Cutlass's shoulder. "You've been very quiet since I put on my glasses," said Captain Cutlass.

Peggle blinked. She watched as the pirates gathered round.

Then Captain Cutlass threw open the lid of the treasure chest.

"Arrrrrrr! Treasure!" cheered the pirates. "Hooray for Captain Cutlass, the pirate who wears glasses!"

"Well, Peggle," said the captain.
"What do you say to that?"
Peggle stared at the pile of glittering
gems and gold. Then she looked at
the smelly pirates. She fluffed up her
feathers and wrinkled her beak...

"Bath time!" squawked the parrot.
The pirates roared with laughter.
"Hold yer beak, Peggle!" said Captain
Cutlass. "Pirates don't take baths!"